For Lex, Ginger, Bonny and everlasting George.

Dedicated to Steve McKay 1955-2015,
and memories of laughter, love and loyalty.

Published in 2016 by Melbournestyle Books

Melbournestyle Books
155 Clarendon Street, South Melbourne
Victoria 3205, Australia
www.melbournestyle.com.au

National Library of Australia
Cataloguing-in-Publication entry:

  Coote, Maree, author, illustrator.

  Spellbound: Making pictures with the A-B-C/Maree Coote.

  ISBN: 9780992491727 (hardback)

  1. Typography–Design–Juvenile literature.
  2. English language–Alphabet–Juvenile literature.
  3. Animals–Pictorial works–Juvenile literature
  4. Cities–Pictorial works–Juvenile Literature
  5. Portraits–Pictorial works–Juvenile Literature

  Dewey Number: 421.1

Design by Maree Coote
Printed in China on wood-free paper

10 9 8 7 6 5 4 3 2 1

MELBOURNESTYLE
AUSTRALIA

www.melbournestyle.com.au

ALPHABET-CITY.COM.AU

SPELLBOUND

MAKING PICTURES WITH THE A-B-C

EVERY PICTURE MADE WITH THE LETTERS OF ITS OWN NAME · LETTER ART

COOTE

ABOUT LETTER ART
NOTES FOR TEACHERS & DESIGNERS

TYPOGRAPHIC POETRY

Also known as shape poetry, visual poetry and concrete poetry, Typographic Poetry enhances the meaning of a text through its visual presentation. In literature, the physical attributes of text are usually ignored, but in Typographic Poetry the words not only represent a concept, they also express it visually, as is the case in art. Text becomes something to look at and comprehend aesthetically, not just something to read. Sometimes the aim is to emphasise or expand the idea of the words, and sometimes it is to contrast or even negate what the words express. The essence of the form lies in the tension between these literary and artistic dimensions.

Early forms of hand-drawn typographic embellishment can be found in religious manuscripts of the Middle Ages, which featured decorative gilded letter-forms that literally 'illuminated' the text. Baroque labyrinth poems of the 1600s sometimes displayed text as a maze, requiring interaction from the reader to follow the path of the words. William Blake's illustrated books of the late 1700s featured hand-painted text within the illustrations, again blurring the line between calligraphy and art and amplifying the power of the word.

And, ever since the advent of moveable Letterpress type, designers have explored illustrative typography and shape-setting. Lewis Carroll's *A Mouse's Tale* from *Alice's Adventures in Wonderland* of 1865 is a shape poem in which the paragraph tapers to resemble a mouse's tail.

In the early twentieth century, European Futurists like Filippo Marinetti, and Dadaist artists including Tristan Tzara, rejected the visual functionality of the written word. By unhinging words from their representational role, they made abstract typographic art experiments. The Surrealists followed in the 1950s and 60s, coining the term Concrete Poetry. The word 'concrete' was meant to infer the giving of solid, tangible form to an abstract idea. An exciting graphic expressionism of visual concepts and typographic poems appeared, like Eugen Gomringer's *Schweigen (Silence)* of 1954 which cleverly expressed the idea of an absence of sound,

silence	silence	silence
silence	silence	silence
silence		silence
silence	silence	silence
silence	silence	silence

and Reinhard Döhl's *Apfel (Apple)* of 1965, which conceals a typographic worm in its midst. Most concrete poetry cannot be read aloud, as the text and image must combine to create the work.

Throughout history, this kind of typographic innovation is made possible by the technology of the day—innovations in printing and typesetting—and is driven by the artist's desire to discover new means for creative expression.

LETTER ART

In this new form of Typographic Poetry, I also explore the possibilities of new technology—in this case, computers and digital fonts. But rather than modifying sentence or paragraph shape, I focus only on the manipulation of *individual letters* in composing an image. The result is 'Letter Art'—a kind of alphabetical sculpture, or pictorial anagram, where the subject of the image is created from the letters that spell its very name.

This approach is made possible by the advent of the Apple Macintosh computer. Since 1984, the Mac and its world of fonts has allowed designers to explore and manipulate type in ways that were previously impossible. For me, this has enabled exploration of typography and logotype design that has ultimately led to *Letter Art*.

As in logotype design, the aim of *Letter Art* is to combine only certain relevant letters in a way that will express a visual idea. The designer must try and retry fonts, positions and combinations until a meaningful image is created. The resulting pictogram is a digital echo of the ancient ideograms and hieroglyphs at the very root of all modern alphabets.

Of course, we can draw a letter freehand, or even create bespoke letters that fit a particular shape within a letter artwork. But I have not created any new fonts. I have limited myself to using only those available in my current font suitcase, so as to avoid an otherwise endless choice. In design, limitations can force increased exploration and innovation, and often lead to serendipitous results.

FONTS & TYPOGRAPHY

A study of line and shape is at the root of all typography.

Weight, character and style differ in every font. Whether creating a headline or a logotype, careful font selection is the key to success.

The same applies to *Letter Art.* Fonts have personality, just like people, animals and even architectural styles.

So, for two striped animals, the tiger and the zebra, I selected an 'open' serif font called IGNATIUS. The double-line design gives it a striped effect that makes these designs work (p.62 and 64). Similarly, for the bushranger Edward 'Ned' Kelly (p.99), I selected a font that matches the mood and spirit of frontier times: a bold 'woodblock' style font called **Davison Americana**. The letters are masculine yet embellished and the shapes in this font add a colonial aesthetic to the final design.

Sometimes a single character can evoke an image or feature so clearly that it leads the way to an easy design result. But often the task is a puzzle of assemblage, as letter by letter, the correct spelling is explored in various fonts to achieve the desired result. Both approaches begin a great design challenge.

This book offers three levels of difficulty. First, that of making pictures using *any letters that inspire* and discovering what objects they conjure. Next, the task is made more difficult when bound by using only the letters of the *correct spelling* of the subject's name. And finally, the challenge of both correct spelling and the limit of

only *one font per letter.* The most difficult of all these are portraits, especially those of famous faces we all know. But as we soon learn in the world of design, nothing is ever impossible.

– MAREE COOTE

TYPOGRAPHY BASICS
NOTES FOR BUDDING TYPOGRAPHERS

Begin by learning about LETTERS.
Look carefully at all 26 letters of the alphabet and study the shapes they contain.
Turn them upside-down and back to front. Is an M *always* the same as an
upside-down W? Explore the alphabet until you know it well.

a   g   a   a

There are CAPITAL letters and small letters
There are *curly* letters and straight letters.
There are lots of ways to write the letters of the alphabet.

Try to understand the secret of each letter. What is it that makes a K
still a **K**, even when it looks like this: *K* or this: *k* or this: **K**?
What is the essence of a K? Can you see a K in this picture:

Why are there so many different ways to make the same letters?
Because the *style* of the letter is often used to reflect the *meaning* of the words.
That's what Typography is all about.
These different styles of letter design are called FONTS…

Firstly, there are SERIF fonts and SANS SERIF fonts.
A serif is like a little 'foot':

Sans is *French* for 'without',
so SANS SERIF is a letter *without* a little foot:

Apart from serif and **sans serif**,
there are also *italic* fonts, which are slanted like handwriting,
there are *script* fonts which look like elegant calligraphy,
and there are DISPLAY fonts, which look like fancy signwriting.
Here are some favourite fonts, many of which are
featured throughout this book:

FONTESQUE

DOT MATRIX

DAVISON AMERICANA

GREYTON SCRIPT

BENGUIAT

COOPER BLACK

GIDDYUP

BERNHARD MODERN

IGNATIUS

SCHMELVETICA

KLUNDERSCRIPT

FRITZ QUADRATA

Different shaped letters are called FONTS. They can be fat or thin, big or small, straight or curly, loud or quiet. They may spell the same words, but they each speak their own design language.

DICOT MEDIUM

MADRONE

LUCIDA HANDWRITING

CURLZ

CENTURY GOTHIC

ANTIQUE OLIVE NORD

HELVETICA NEUE

SLOOP

HANDEL GOTHIC

LAMBADA

SCRIPT MT BOLD

CALAVERA 2

ANGLIA OLD ENHANCEMENTS

INDUSTRIA

SPELLBOUND

The letters of the alphabet
are made up of *shapes.*
Cities are also made up of *shapes.*

If you keep the A-B-C in mind,
you will start to recognise
shapes in architecture all around you.

You will **notice** letter shapes
in all kinds of things like
buildings, bridges, trains, bikes
and everyday objects.

Sideways, backwards, upside-down,
the alphabet's all over town...

ARCHITEXT

The Rules

There are 3 levels of difficulty in LETTER ART:

1. BEGINNERS: Use *any* letters *any* way. Be **inspired** by the letter's shape.

2. ADVANCED: Use *only* the letters found in the **correct spelling** of the name of the picture you are making. You can use multiple fonts and repeat letters.

Look for patterns and texture in the architecture around you.

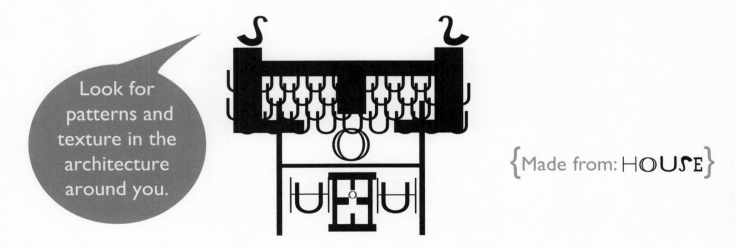

3. DESIGNERS: Use *only the correct spelling* and only **one font per letter**. You can repeat letters if necessary, or make it EXTRA HARD with *no repeats*!

Getting started. Find these letters in the trees...

rlTOYQ SYD **g** BOY

Find these letters in the house below...

AAHHHiHDBEEiOi

BEGINNERS make a house using *any* letters you like.

{ E + H + B = window with curtain }

Which letters can you see in the house nextdoor?

MIANSION

This house is made from the letters that spell its name:

GinGERBREAD HOUSE

{ D + E = door with hinges }

TERRACED HOUSE

Back-to-front or *upside-down*,
All these letters can be found.

Some homes are made from converted warehouses.
Even **simple** architecture contains lots of *alphabetical inspiration*.

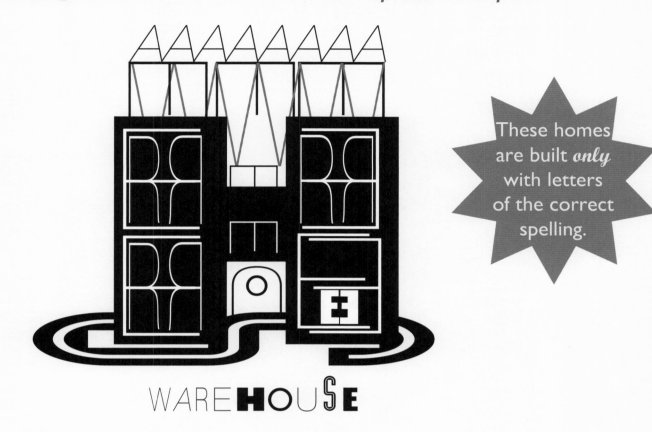

These homes are built *only* with letters of the correct spelling.

WARE**HOU**S**E**

Victorian terrace houses have lots of intricate *surface detail*.
Can you find all the letters *hidden* in this row of terraces?

TERRACE HOUSES

What *shapes* can you find in the architecture of *your* city?

These buildings are built with *any letters* that inspire...

This Chinese Pagoda is made *only* with the letters of its name.

CHINESE PAGODA

Observe details like:
domes
spires
turrets
gables
steps
eaves
verandahs
gargoyles
railings
archways
columns...

Look at the city around you. Look at the letters of the alphabet.
Which letters **remind** you of the piers of a bridge?
An arched doorway? A row of columns?
Which letters inspire a spire?

These trees and plants are made *only* from the letters that spell...

...ROYAL BOTANIC GARDENS

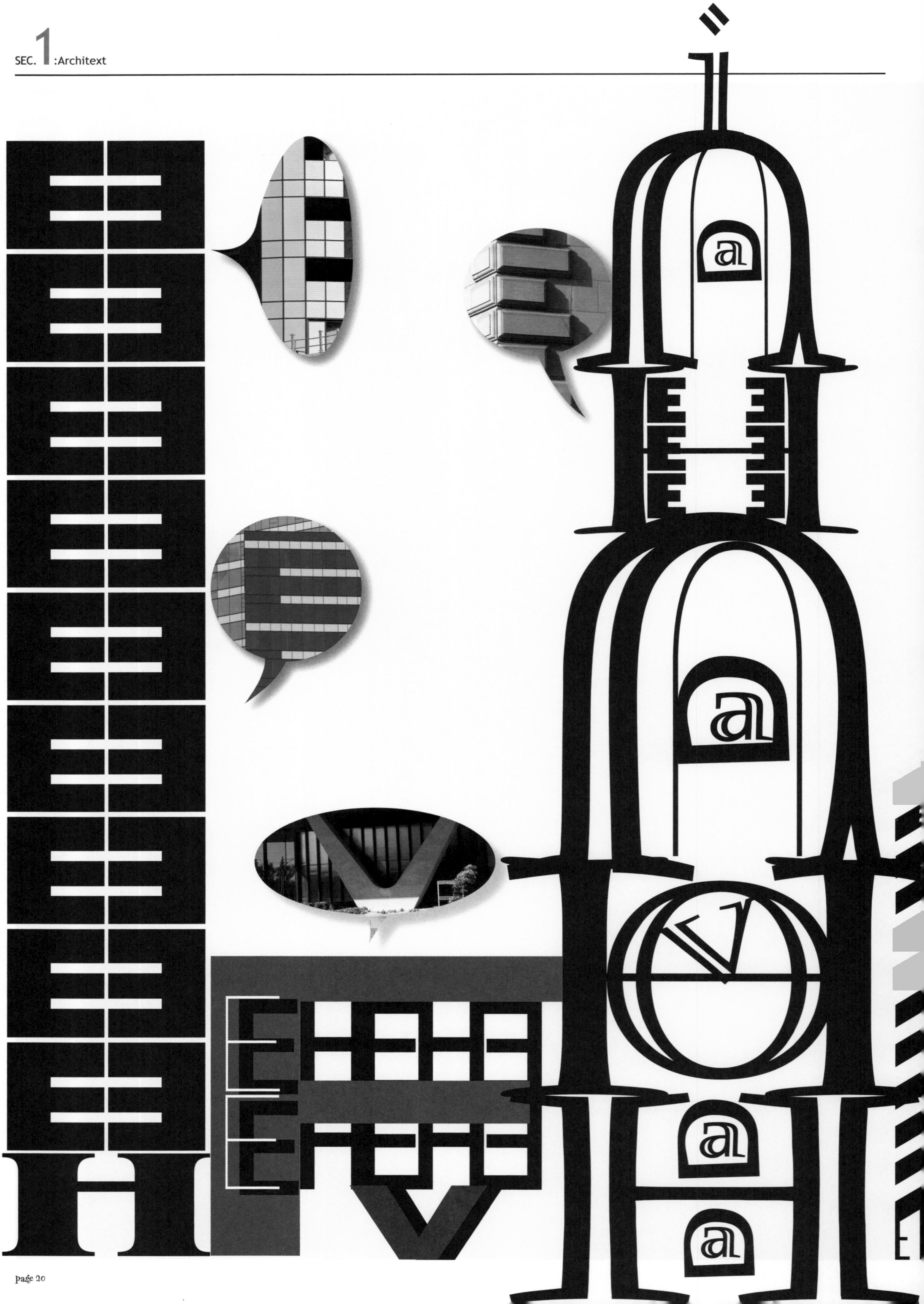

What letters can you find in **your** city?
Next time you go to town, observe the *shapes* in architecture...
In modern buildings that are tall and straight, you can see
the simple shapes of SANS SERIF letters like **L** or **E**.
In old-style buidlings, you can see shapes
that resemble SERIF FONT letters like **U** or **H**.

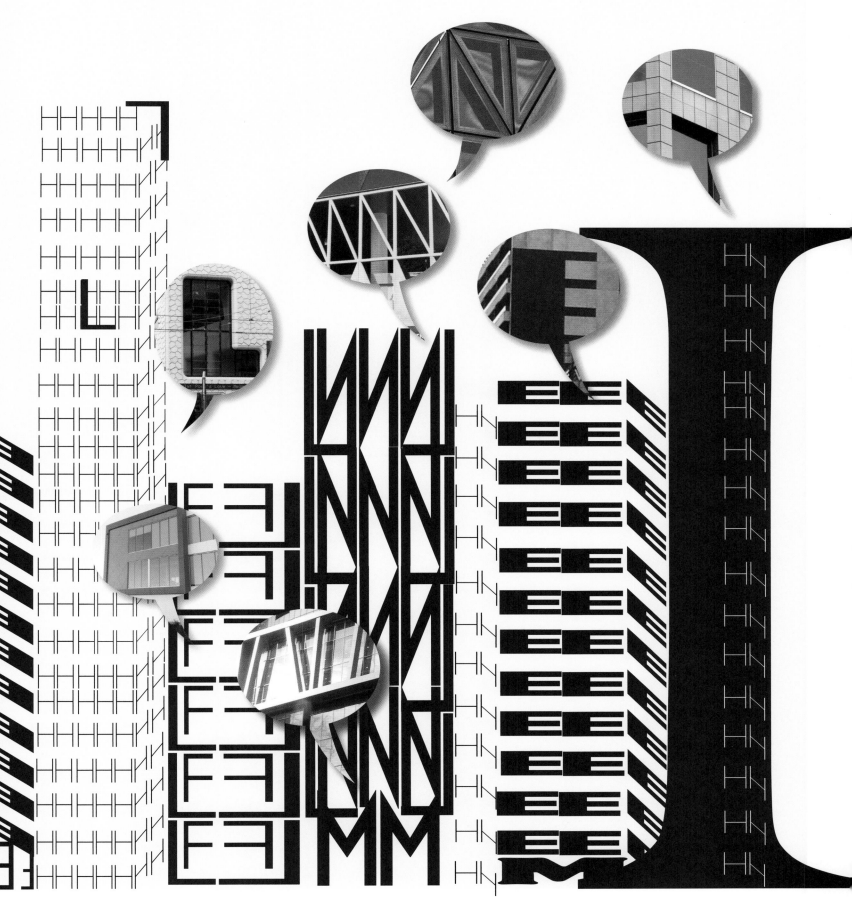

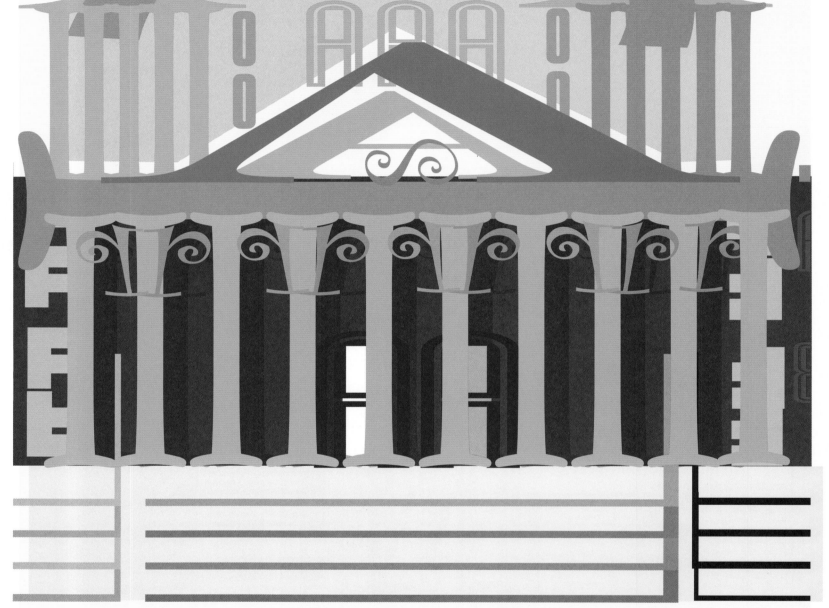

STATE LIBRARY OF VICTORIA

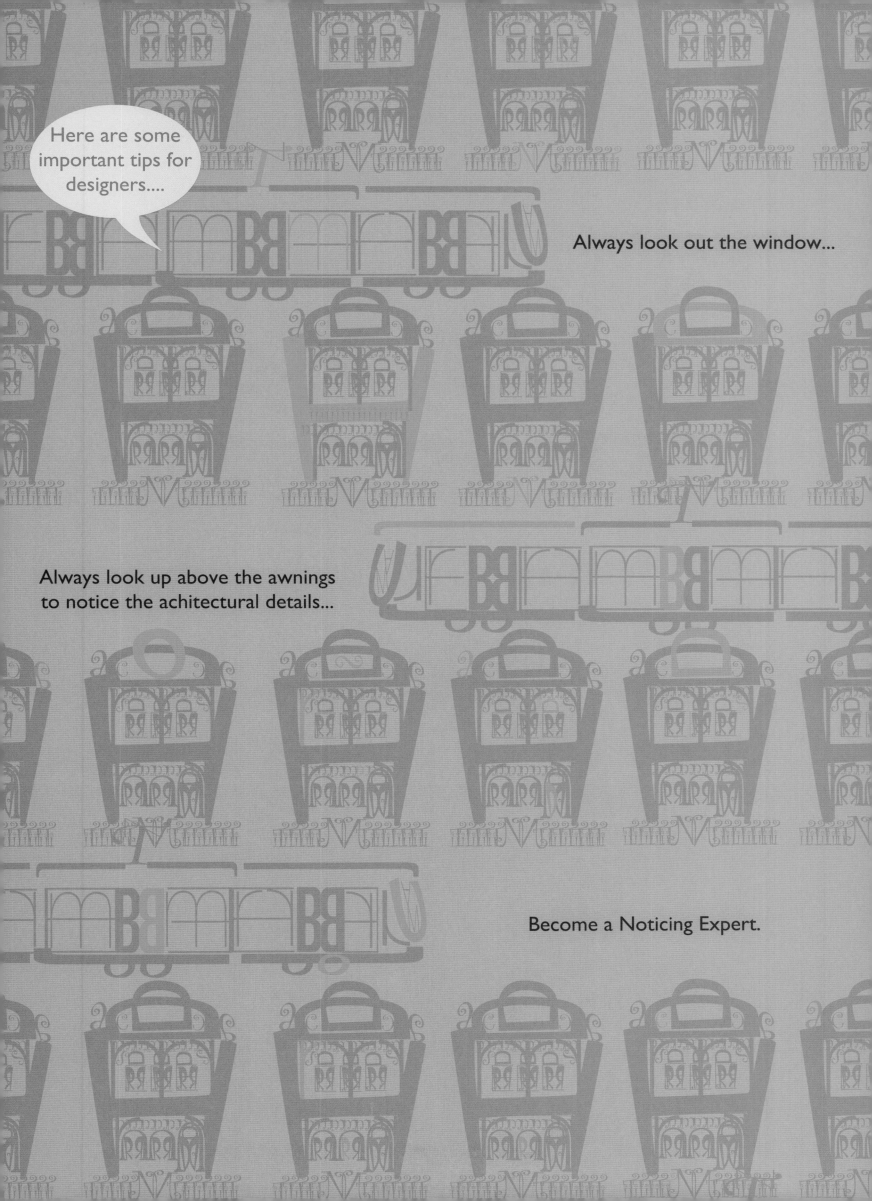

What letters hide in the buildings of London, Sydney and New York?

SYDNEY OPERA HOUSE

These landmarks are made *only* from the letters of their name.

LONDON EYE

CHRYSLEr BUILDinG

The R, G, S, I and i from
the letters above are
used to make the
eagle head gargoyles:

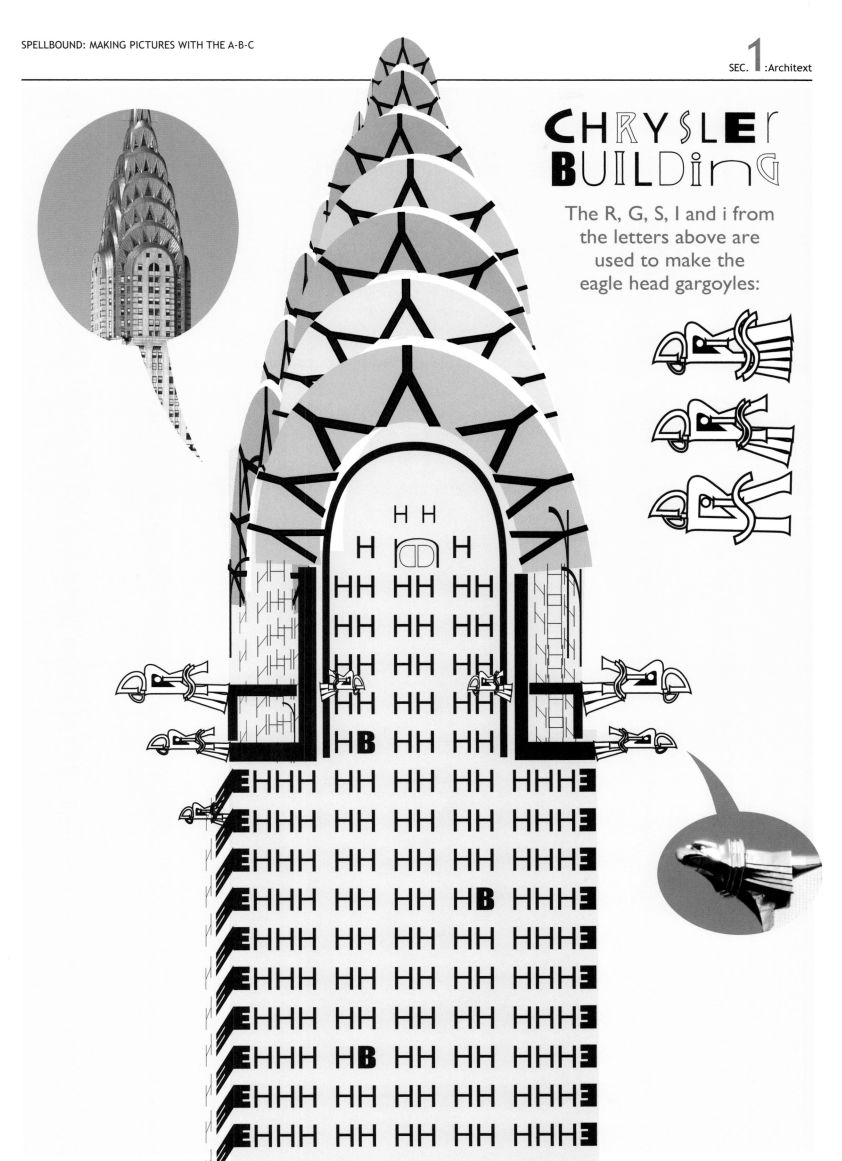

There are *old-fashioned* and **modern** trams in Melbourne.
This is a modern tram, made from these letters:

MELBOURNE TRAM

Right-way-up or
wrong-way-round,
All the letters
can be found.

The 1923 **W Class** tram is Melbourne's favourite.
It's made of *wood* and has a green and gold colour scheme.

MELBOURNE TRAM

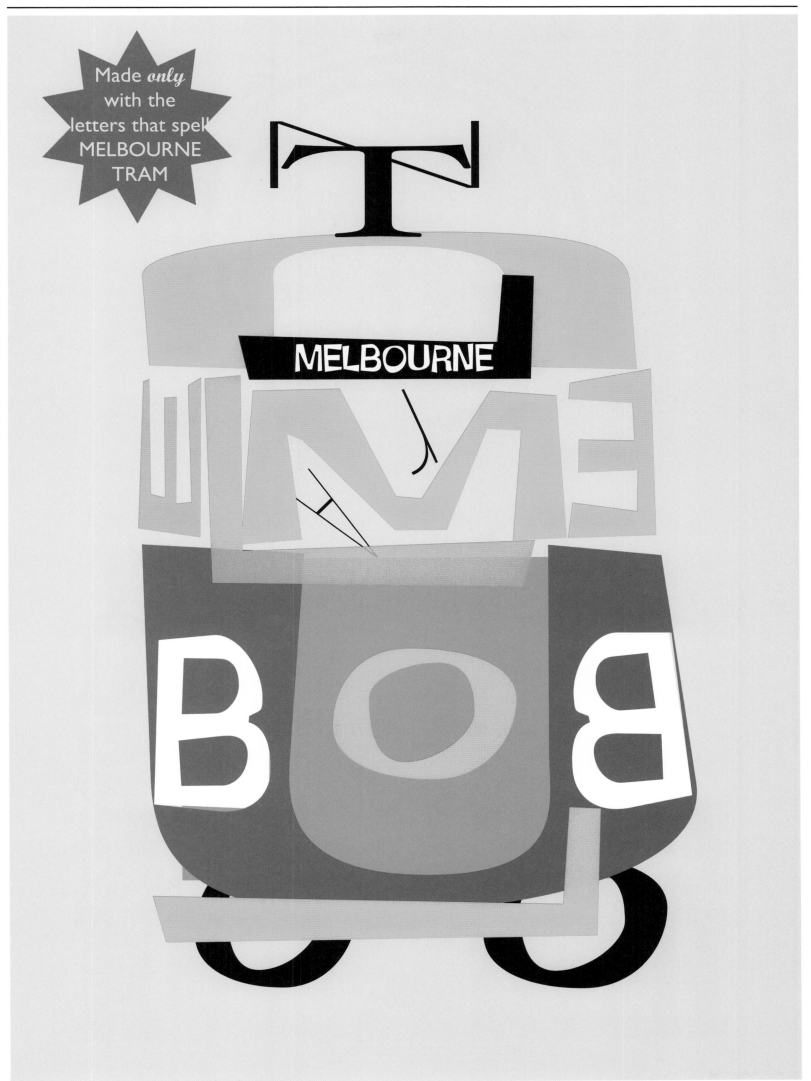

Made *only* with the letters that spell MELBOURNE TRAM

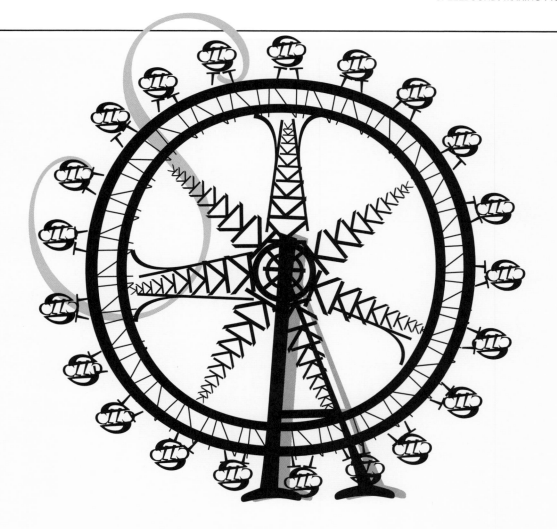

DOCKLANDS STAR

There'll *probably* be a big wheel in your city –
can you find letter shapes in its design?
No wheel? What letters can you see
in your local Town Hall?

MELBOURNE TOWN HALL

The city of Bologna
is famous for its *towers*
and covered *arcade* footpaths.
BOLOGNA, ITALIA

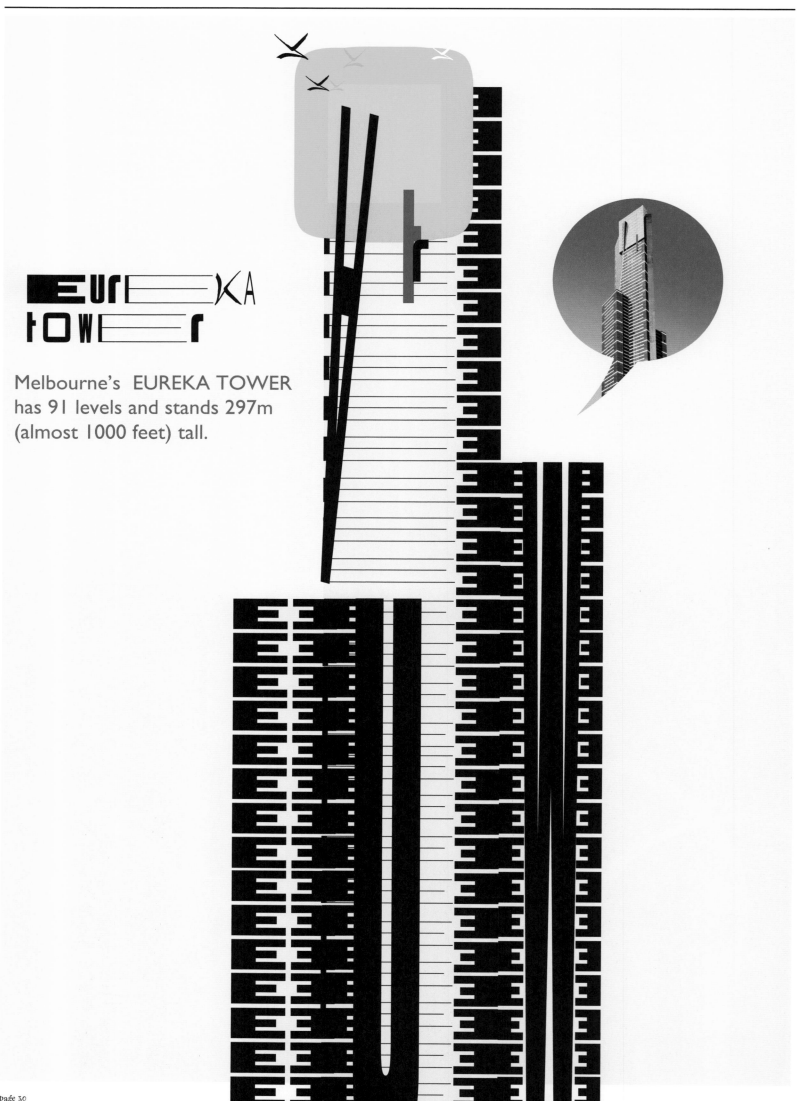

EUREKA TOWER

Melbourne's EUREKA TOWER
has 91 levels and stands 297m
(almost 1000 feet) tall.

BIG BEN
is the *nickname* given
to the clock in the tower
of the Palace of
Westminster, London.

For *St Paul's Cathedral*, capital A's are an obvious choice for the spires.
The apostophe (ˌ) is used to create the dotty edge detail of the spires.
Rose windows are made of C's, and gothic window and doors
are made from *upside-down* U's and detail is added with E's.

St PAUL'S CAtHEDRAL

Study the building in **sections**:
The entrance of FLINDERS STREET STATION
is made from capital F's in a font with a traditional style.
The *decorative* features are made from *decorative* fonts.
The steps are made from a stack of capital L's.

FLinDers STREET STATION

STREET STATION

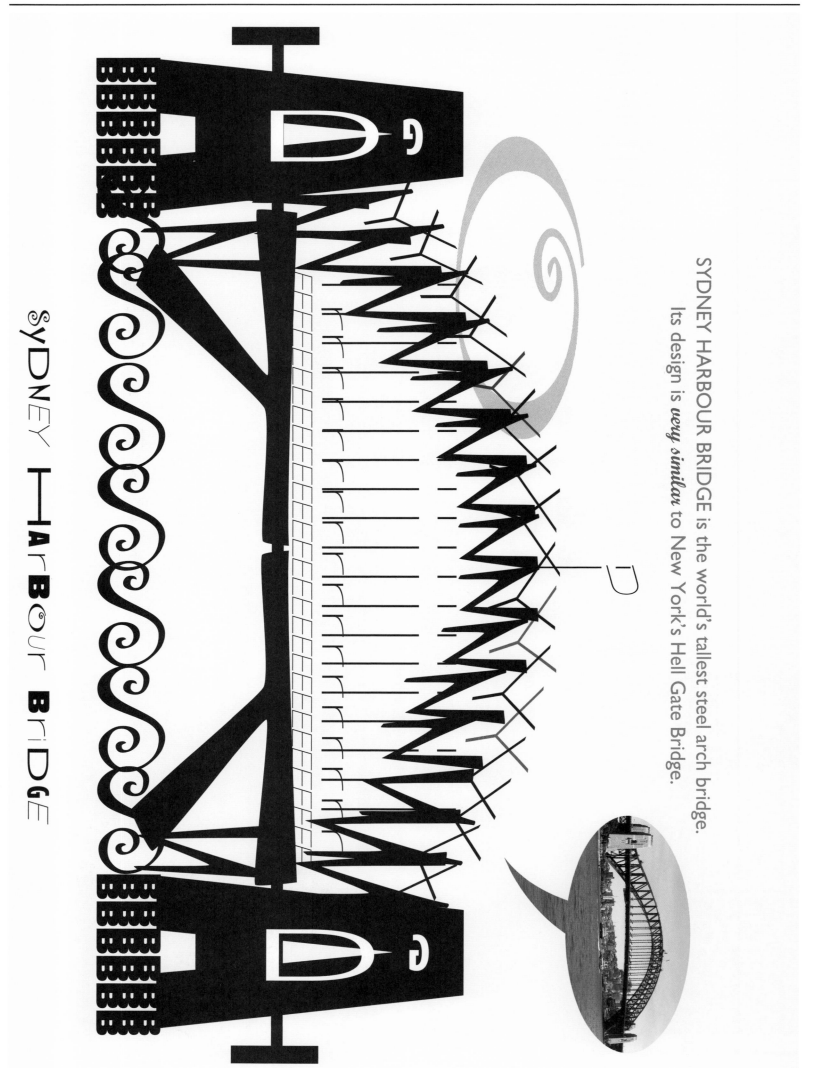

SYDNEY HARBOUR BRIDGE

SYDNEY HARBOUR BRIDGE is the world's tallest steel arch bridge.
Its design is *very similar* to New York's Hell Gate Bridge.

Luna Park has hundreds of exciting
shapes and colours in its facade,
but only has *eight* letters in its name,
so letters must be used in *different ways*
to create the picture.

LUNA PARK

FLINDERS STREET STATION

SPELLBOUND

Animals
are also made up of *shapes*.

Observe them with the
A-B-C in mind
and you will start to notice
letter *shapes* in
snouts, eyes, cheeks,
ears, tails, horns...

(Remember, letters might repeat
to make more eyes or legs or feet,
A letter might be multiplied
to make a patterned fur or hide.)

ALPHABEASTS

Purrfect! Now here's the game: Find the letters of my name.

Can you see what I am made of?

C C A a A t

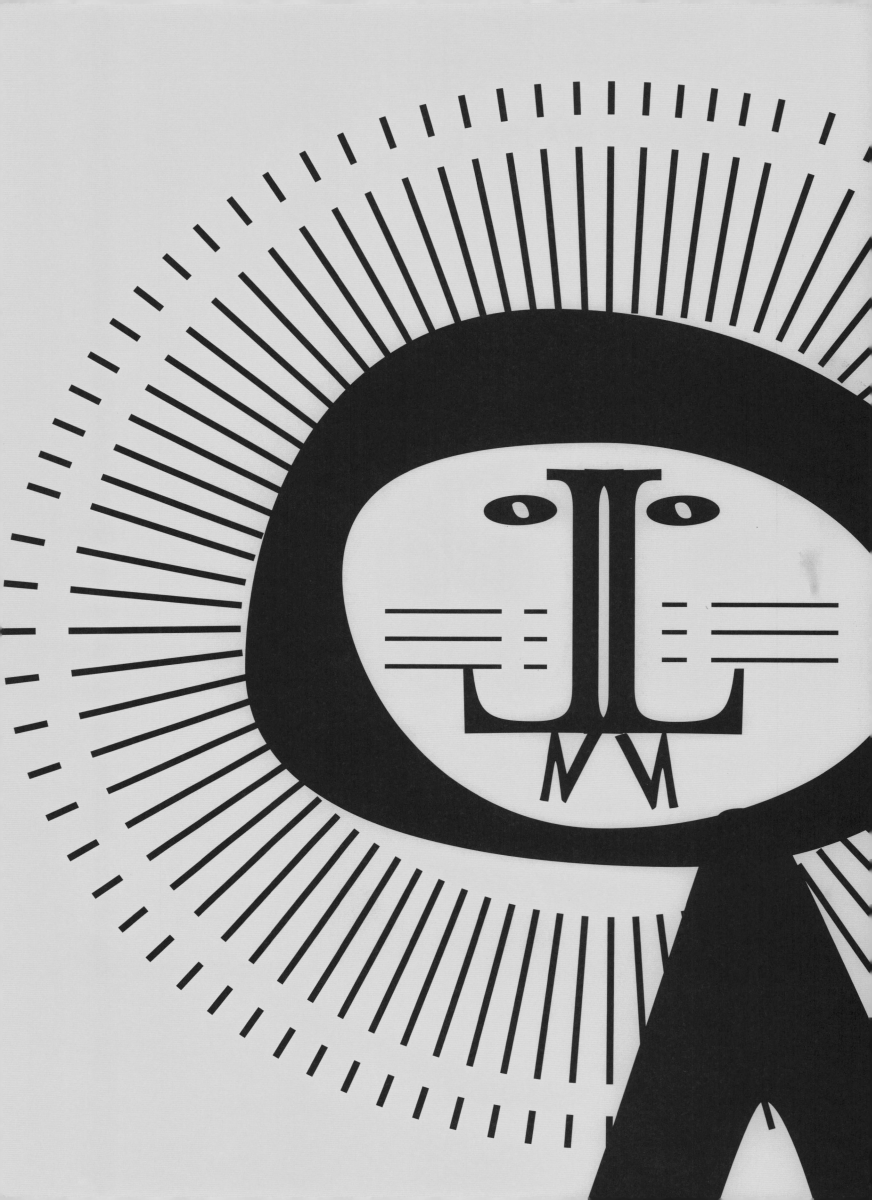

The Rules

There are 3 levels of difficulty in LETTER ART:

{Made from: OwgergMw}

I. BEGINNERS: Use *any* letters, *any* way. Be **inspired** by the letter's shape to make an animal or feature. Repeat letters if you like.

{Made from: CacAat}

meow

2. ADVANCED: Use *only* letters found in the **correct spelling** of the name of the animal in the picture. You can use multiple fonts and repeat letters.

{Made from: Cat}

3. DESIGNERS: Use *only the correct spelling* and only **one font per letter**. You can repeat letters if necessary, or make it EXTRA HARD with *no repeats!*

Getting started. There are lots of ways to make an animal.
An O makes an easy circular head, and e's can make good eyes:

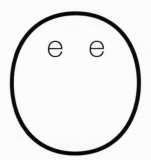  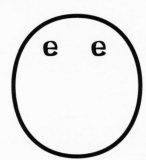

Next comes a nose or **snout**. The letter D on its side makes a great snout,
and works well *combined* with a Y or an A:

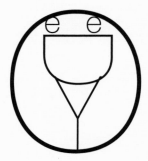  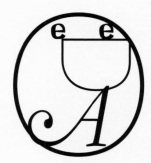

Add a pair of **ears**. The letter A is great for ears and so is C,
but remarkably, almost *any letter* will work for almost *any feature*.

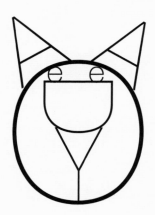  

Look at your **toys** – can you see any letter shapes in their faces?
Do their body shapes remind you of letters?
Remember, letters could be *hiding* upside down or back to front.

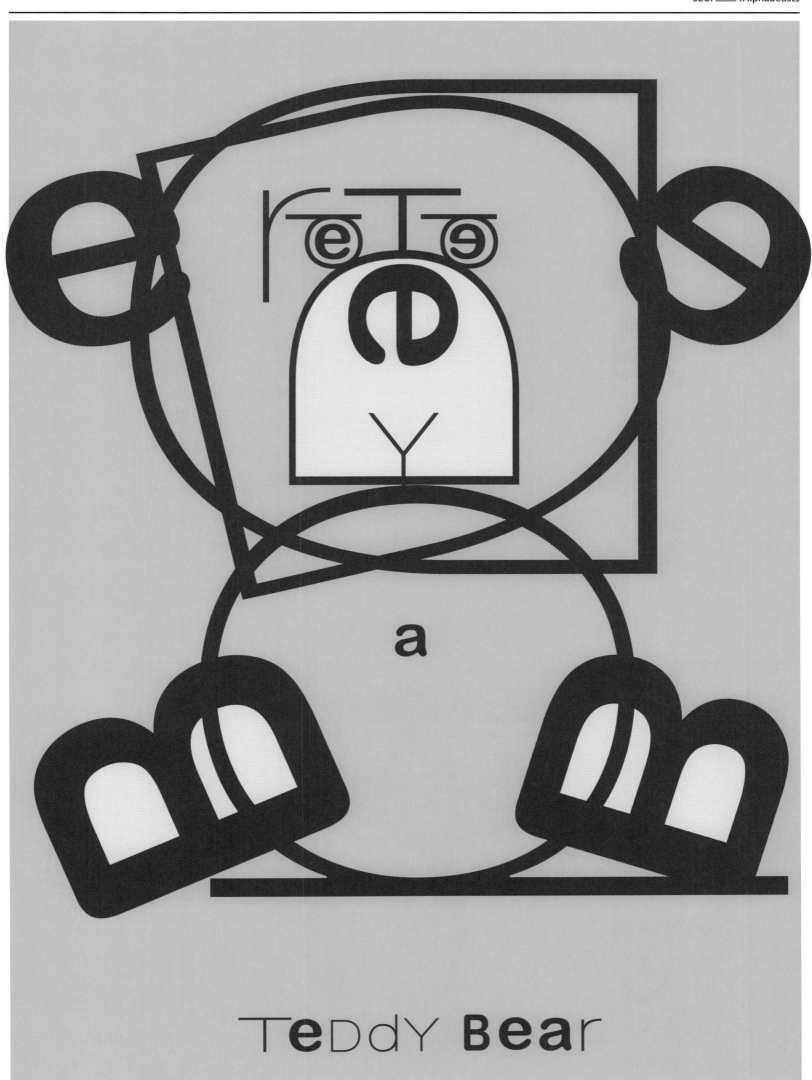

TeDdY Bear

These pictures use *only* **the letters of the animal's name:**

CCAat   CAaaAT   MOGGY

Short words like C-A-T can be hard, so using *more than one font*
provides more letters and shapes, or *repeat some letters* for eyes and ears.
Also, if we give the cat a **nickname** like MOGGY or PUSS,
there are even more letters to work with.

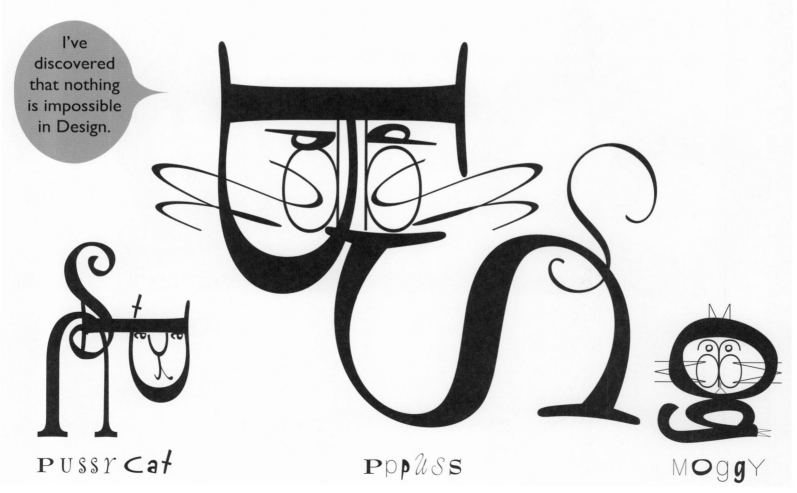

PUSSYCat   PPpUSS   MOGGY

c c A a t

This cat is exactly the *same design* recipe as the one below.
It uses the same letters in the same places. The only difference is the **font** choice.
A *script* font A (above) makes the whiskers more *whiskery*,
and the serif font C for a head and a for the body make the cat look more
tapered and elegant than the blunt shapes of the sans serif fonts below:

c C A a t

Time for a dog show!

Find the letters in the art, It's easy once you make a start.

{ Made from: **DOG** }

Let's try D-O-G. (*Repeat* some letters for extra ears or eyes).

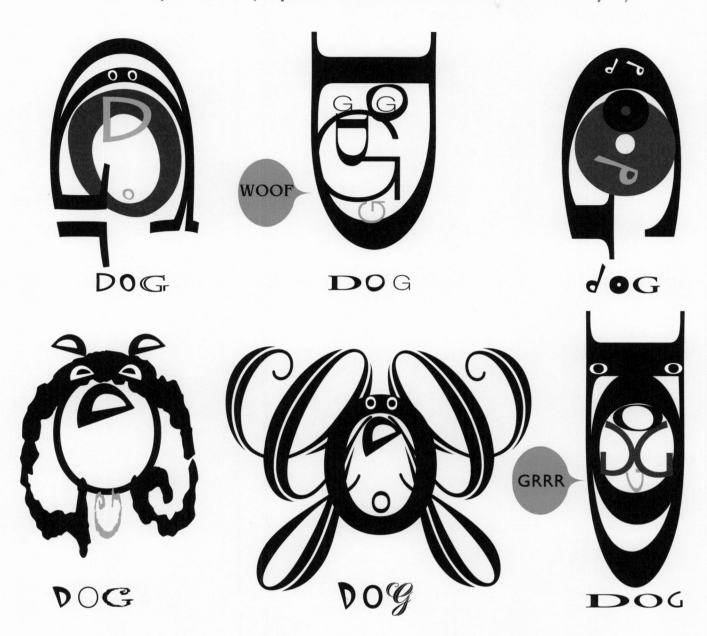

Exaggerate the most **striking feature**: A big nose? Droopy eyes? Silky fur?
Make it D-O-G-G-Y to get that extra letter Y — it's great for a snout.

Sometimes letters might repeat (to make extra wings or feet)
but basically we're four-letter birds. Can you match us to our words?

biRD
BiRD
biRd
biRD
Bird
biRD

MAGPIE

Can you *match* these **bugs** to the letters they are made of?

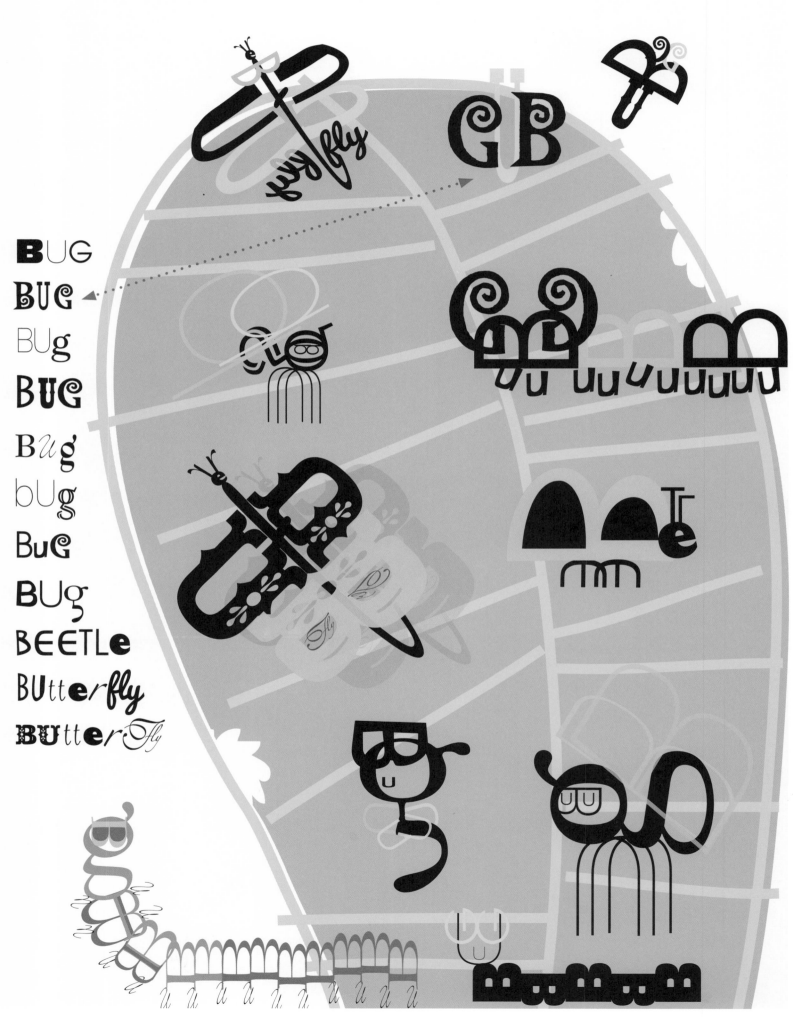

BUG
BUG
BUg
BUG
Bug
bUg
BuG
BUg
BEETLe
BUtterfly
BUtterfly

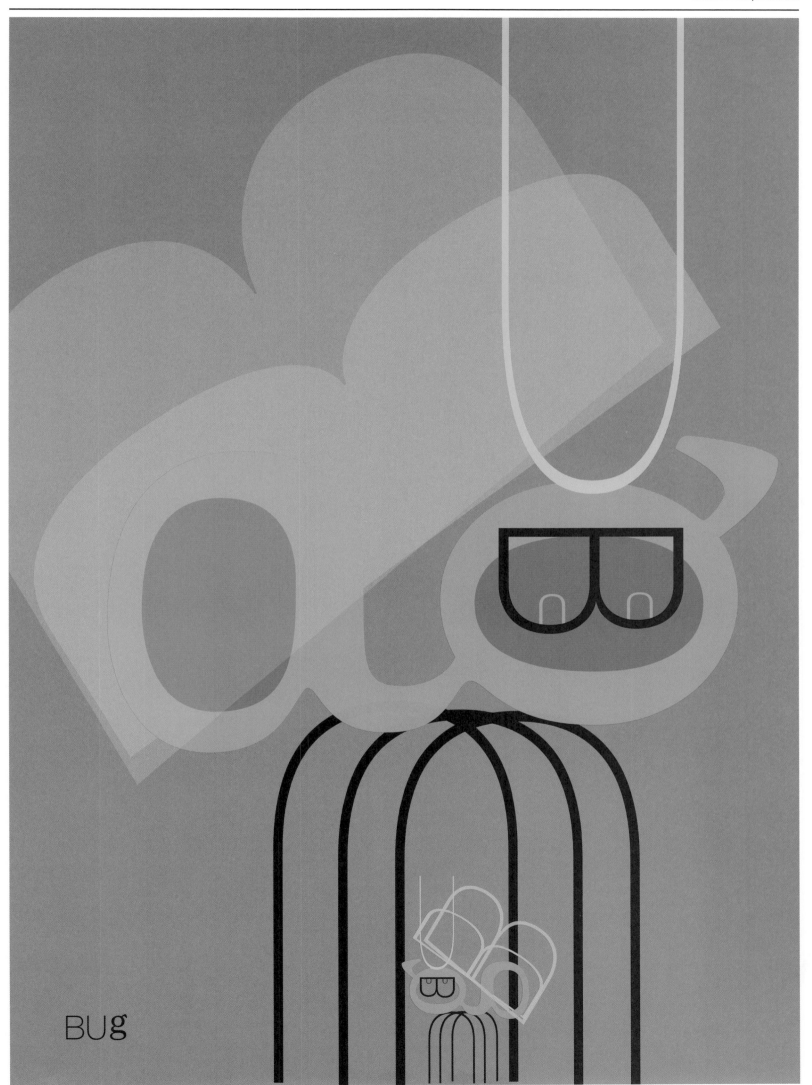

BUg

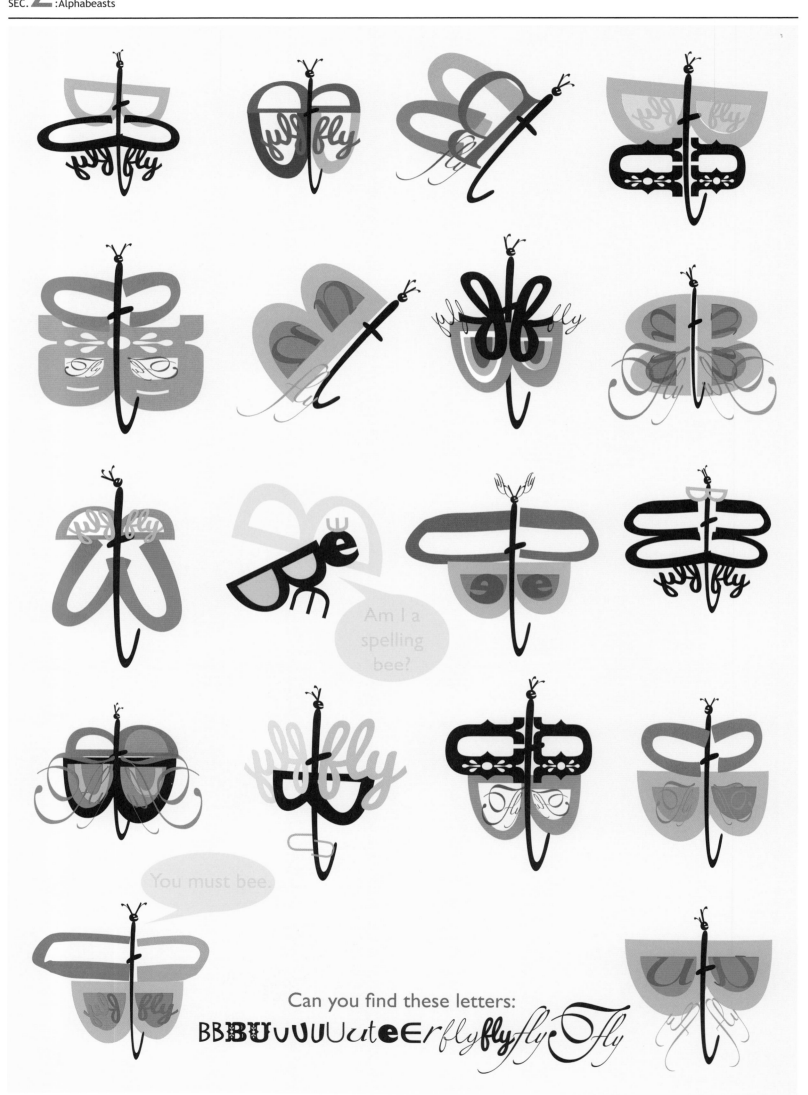

Am I a
spelling
bee?

You must bee.

Can you find these letters:
BBBU∪∪∪∪∪uteEr flyflyfly Fly

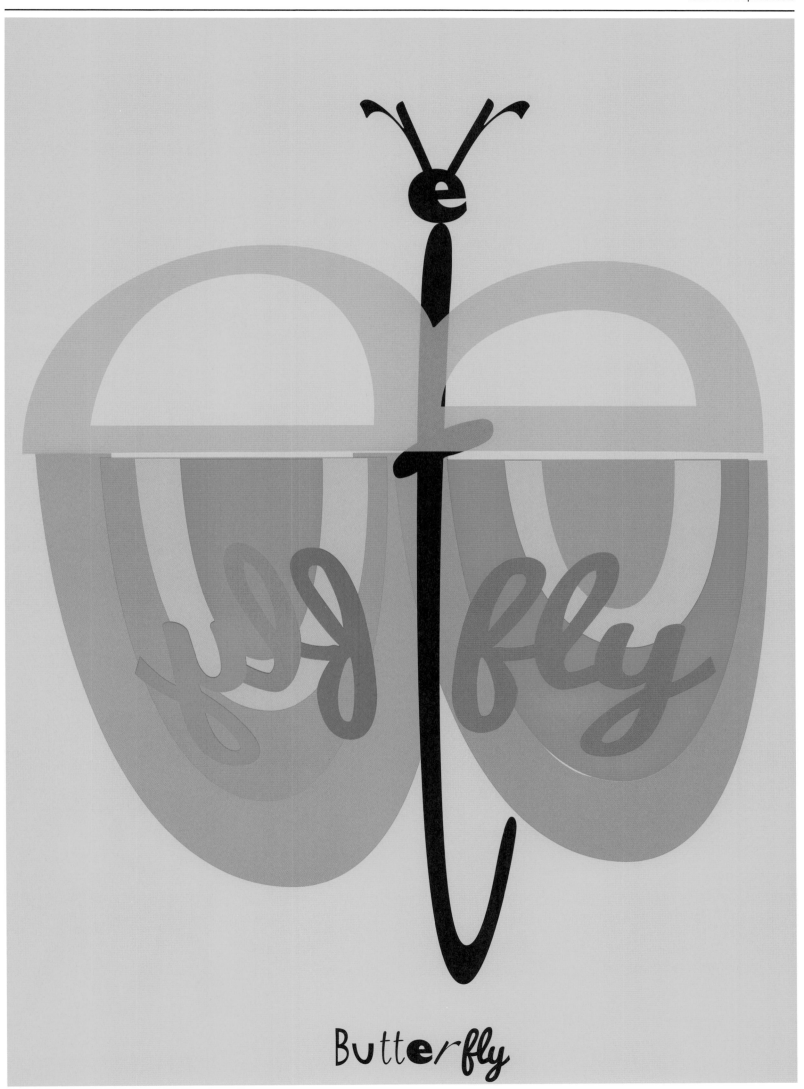

Butterfly

Exaggerating a key feature like **ears** or **horns** gives an animal more graphic impact.

That cow is made with an extra *w* in an udder font (joke).

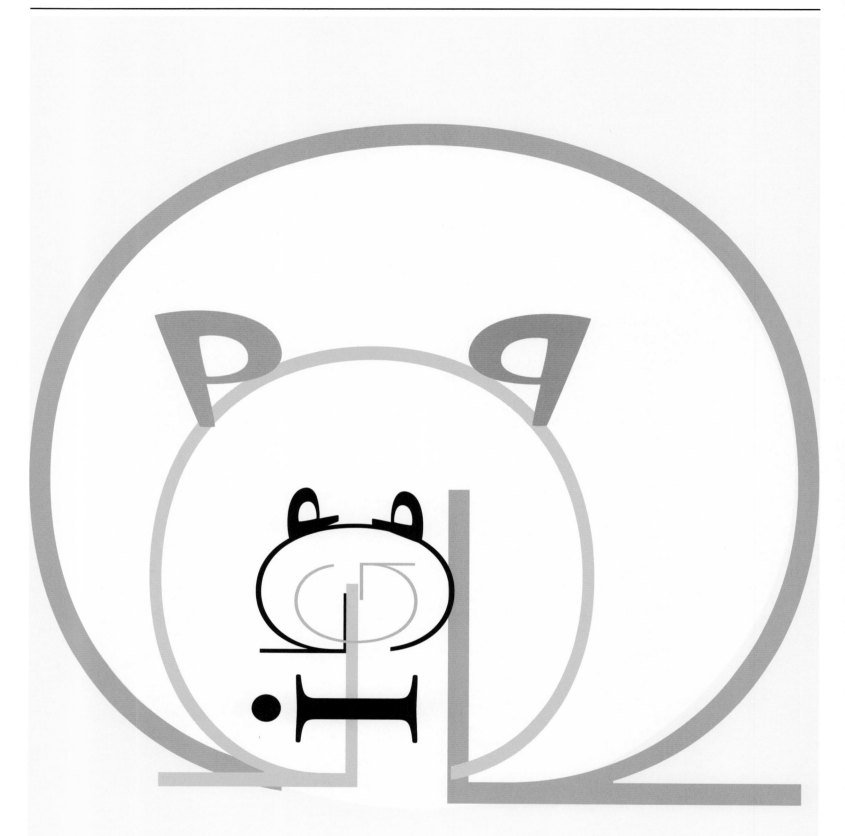

What's the **piggiest** thing about a pig?
Is it the *snouty* snout? The *curly* tail? The *hoofy* hooves?
The *hammy* hocks? The *fatty* face? Or the *piggy* eyes?
Try different fonts for these three little letters. Move the ears around,
change the eyes... get a feel for the way **typography** changes the pig.

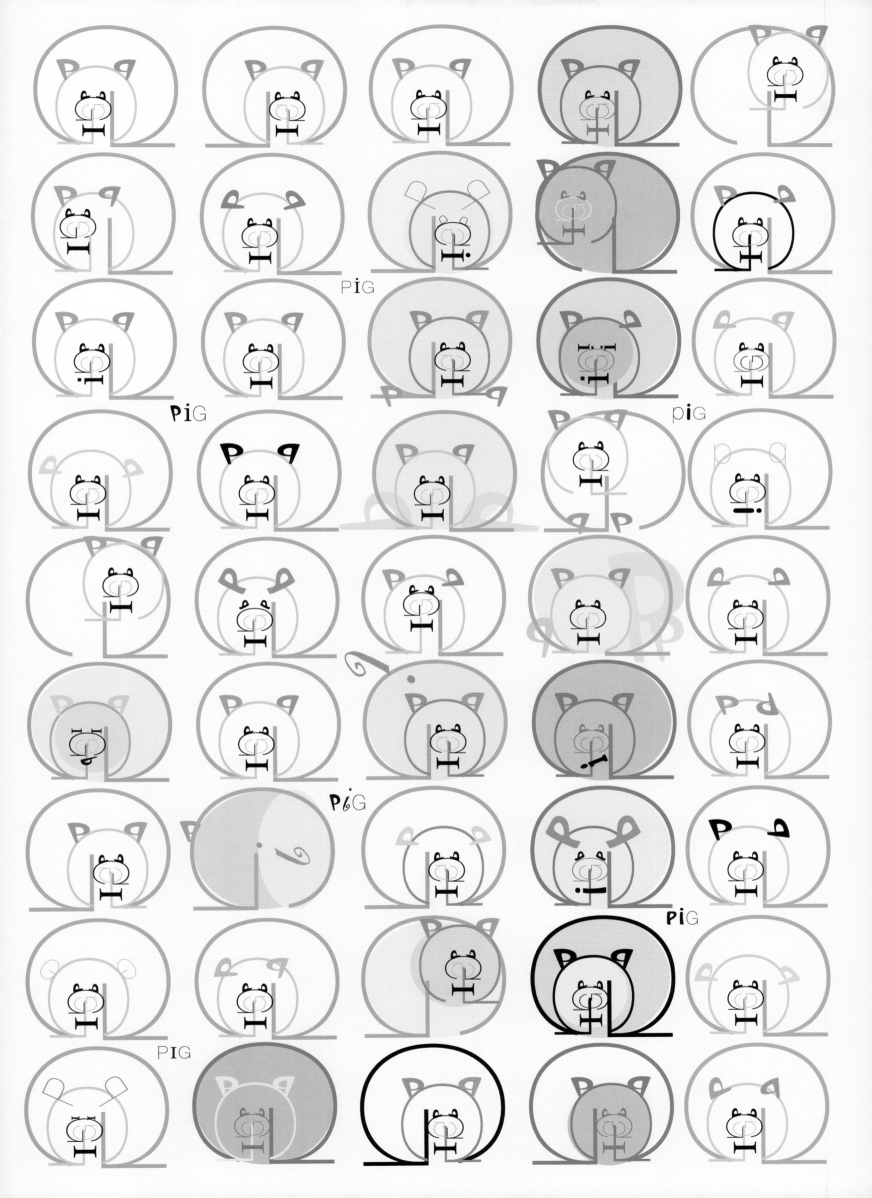

LiON

LiONE§S

Spell a *picture*
not a **word?**
That's the craziest
thing I've heard!

tigeR
{ Face made from: g+*e*+i }

LIONESS

A pack of lions *is called a* PRIDE

Lenny Lion

LiON

King of the jungle
wears a crown:
CROWN

LEO Lion

Back-to-front or
upside-down,
All these letters
can be found:
ZebrA

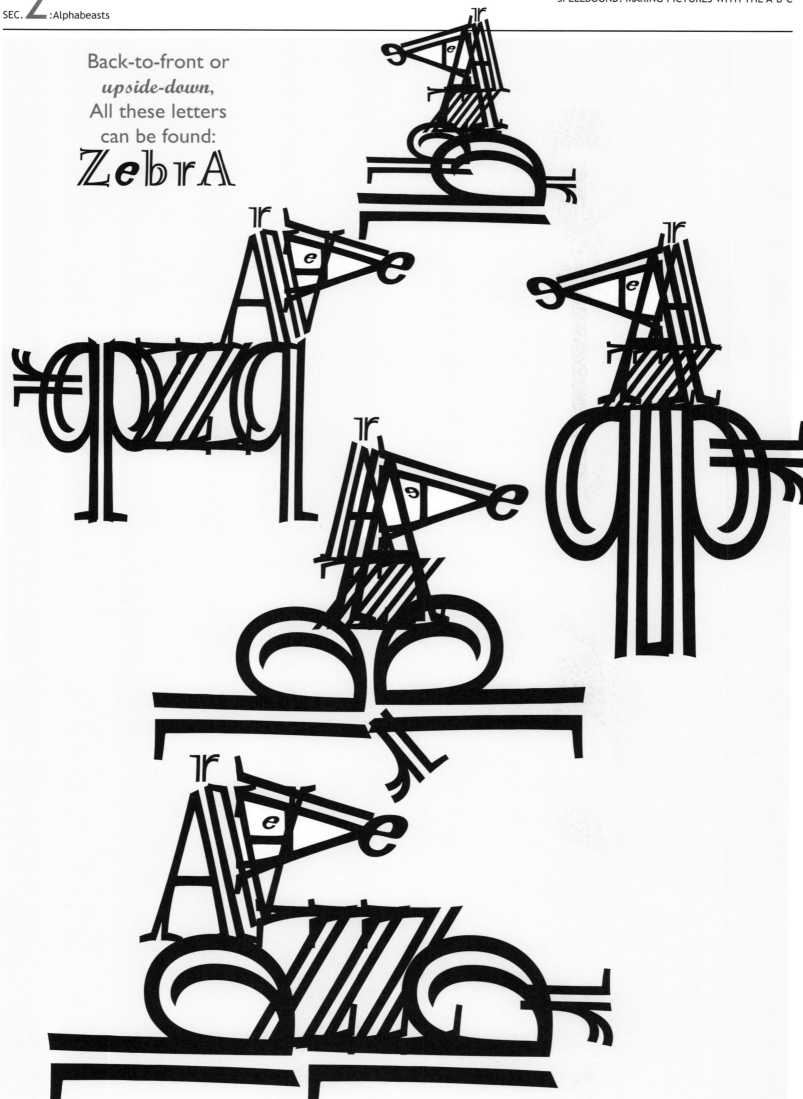

In the zoo, the game's the same: *find the letters* of my name.

Study the *body language* of the animal.
Pandas sit in a lazy slouch.

PanDa

Nobody makes a monkey outta me.

Orang = man
Utan = forest
Orangutan means
'man of the forest'.

ORANGUTAN

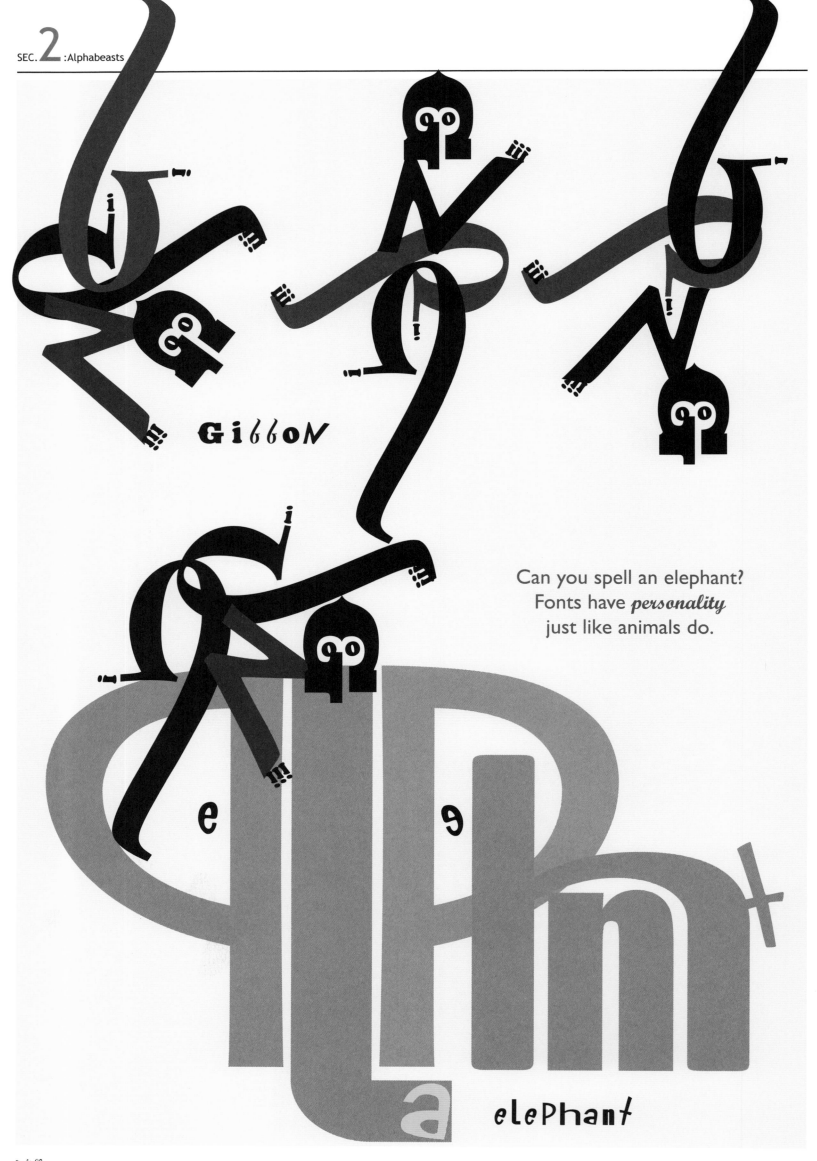

Gibbon

Can you spell an elephant?
Fonts have *personality*
just like animals do.

elephant

Sometimes letters might *repeat*,
to make the picture more complete,
creating pattern, hair or fur
to make giraffes *giraffier.*

ENOUGH!
Too much
monkey business!

giraffe

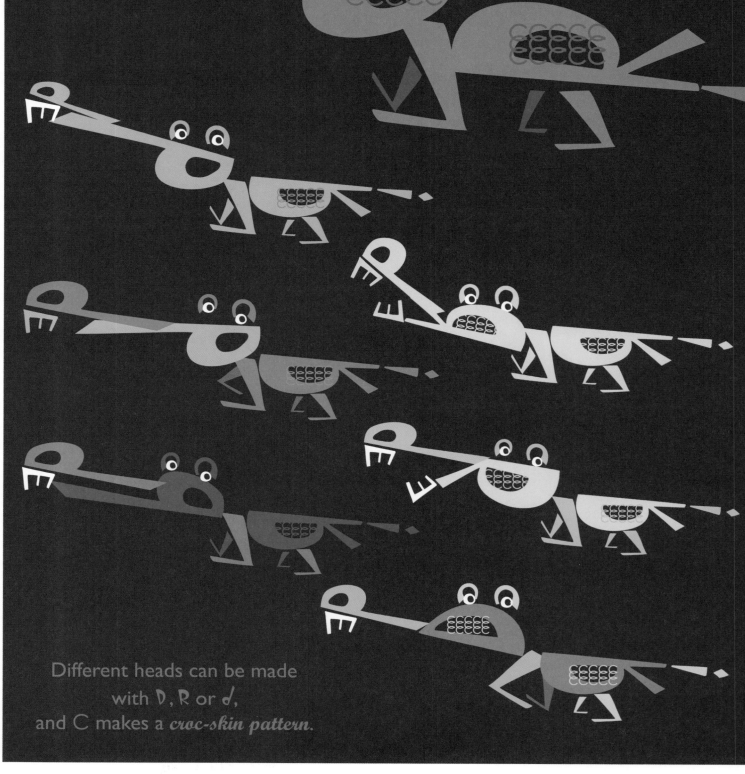

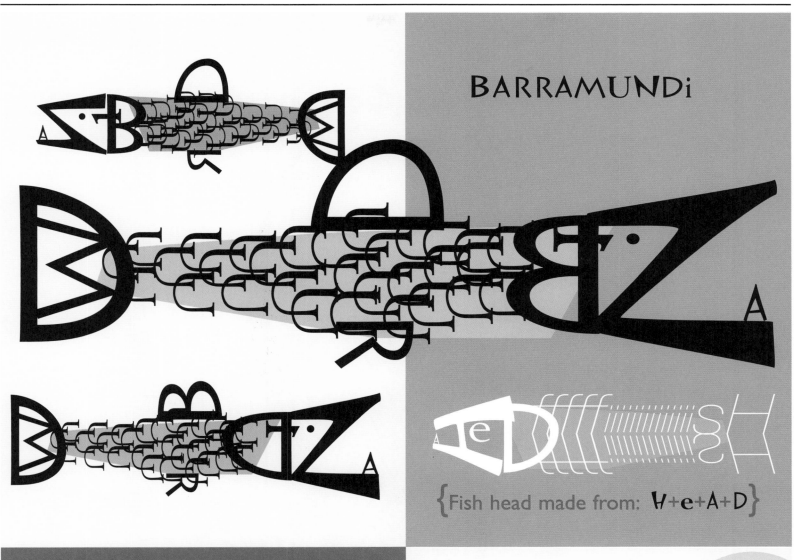

BARRAMUNDi

{Fish head made from: V+e+A+D}

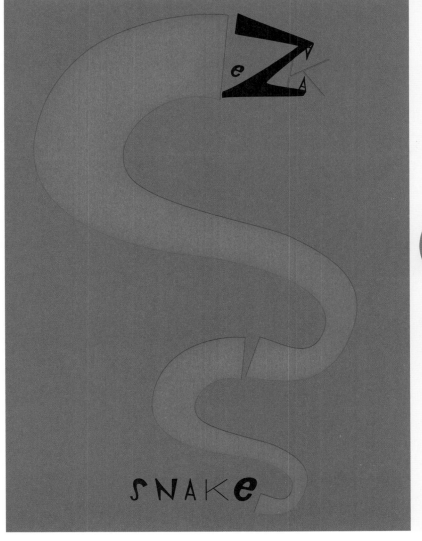

SNAKe

Spell each creature, Find its name, It's an *alphabetical* game.

OCTOPUS

Birds are full of *design inspiration* – study their feathers, beaks and plumes.
Can you *find the letters* that make these birds?

Toucan Macaw Parrot

Invent your own **fantasy** bird... It doesn't have to be real.

PEACOCK

A different *font* makes a different Koala.

Koala

koala

A Koala is not a bear.

I can't bear it.

Koala

KOALA

Can you find these letters in the picture?

koaLa

Different letters for wings and eyes make a *different* kookaburra.

KOoKABURRA

KOoKAbURRA

A baby kangaroo is
called a **joey**...
Can you find the letters
in these pictures?

KANGAROo + JOey

Find and *unscramble* the **hidden** letters to discover the name of each object in the picture.

SPELLBOUND

The *shapes* of the letters of the Alphabet
can even be found in **Faces**.

See if you can recognise letter shapes
in eyes, lips, ears and noses...

The trick with any portrait is to express
the most *striking* feature
and to capture a likeness of the subject.
Remember, fonts have **character**
and personality, just like people do.

LETTERHEADS

Yo Ho Hum.

Can you find these letters in this pirate face?

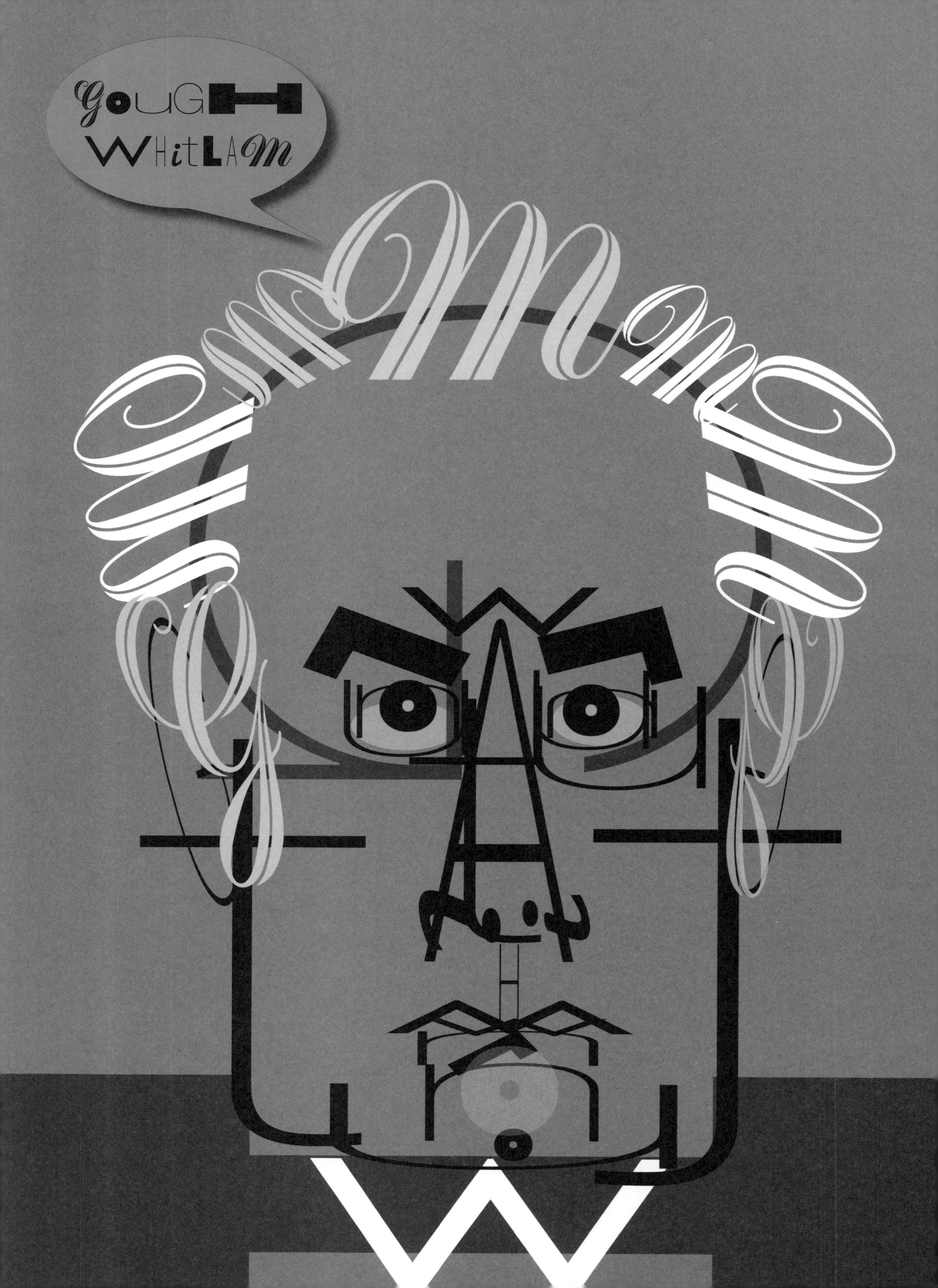
Gough Whitlam

The Rules

There are 3 levels of difficulty in LETTER ART:

{Made from: *awƐgOe*}

1. BEGINNERS: Use *any* letters you like. Be **inspired** by the letter's shape to make a certain feature. Repeat letters if you like.

{Made from: **you**U}

2. ADVANCED: Use *only* letters found in the **correct spelling** of the name of the portrait you are making. You can repeat letters in multiple fonts.

I'm not as simple as I look.

{Made from: **yo**U}

3. DESIGNERS: Use *only the correct spelling* and only **one font per letter**. You can repeat letters if necessary, or make it EXTRA HARD with *no repeats*!

Faces with character... Here are the basics:

The letter O starts off an *easy* face.
The position of the letters *inside* the O creates different expressions.

Just about *any* letter can become *any* feature. The letter **d** on its side makes
a great mouth (above), but it also makes eyes with built-in eyebrows (below).

Look at the faces in your family. Look for the letter shapes in their faces,
and remember, letters could be sideways, upside-down or even backwards.

There are *lots* of ways to begin a face, and a **chin** is as good a place as any.
Some chins can look like a U, a V or an upside-down A.
Other letters can combine to add double chins or dimples.

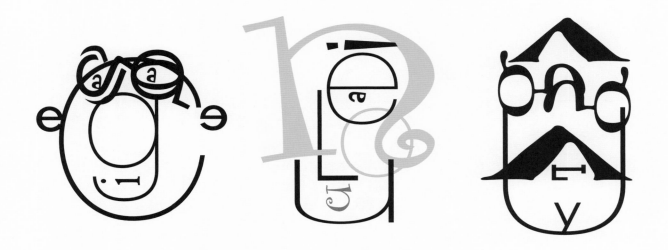

Accessories like *glasses* also contain letter shapes.
The letter B makes a great pair of glasses. Or try a lower case letters
like a, b, d, p or g to make spectacles like these:

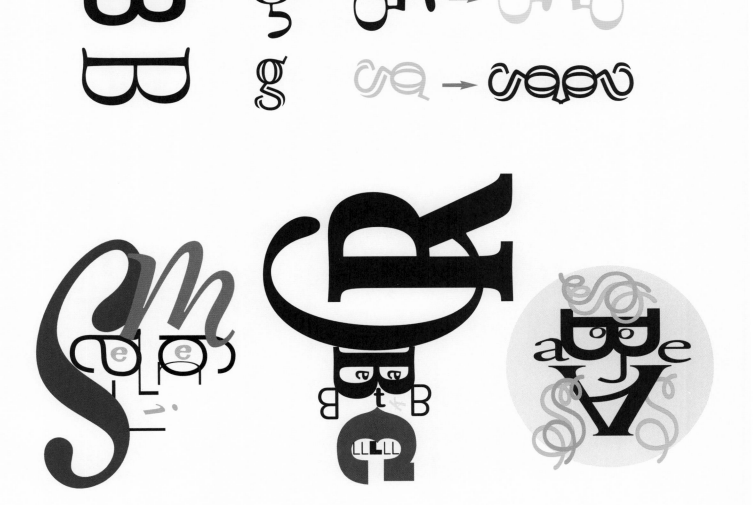

Facial hair is lots of fun: beards and moustaches, sideburns and goatees.
Dotty letters make the beard look *bristley*.
All the faces below are made with the same letters – only the facial hair changes...

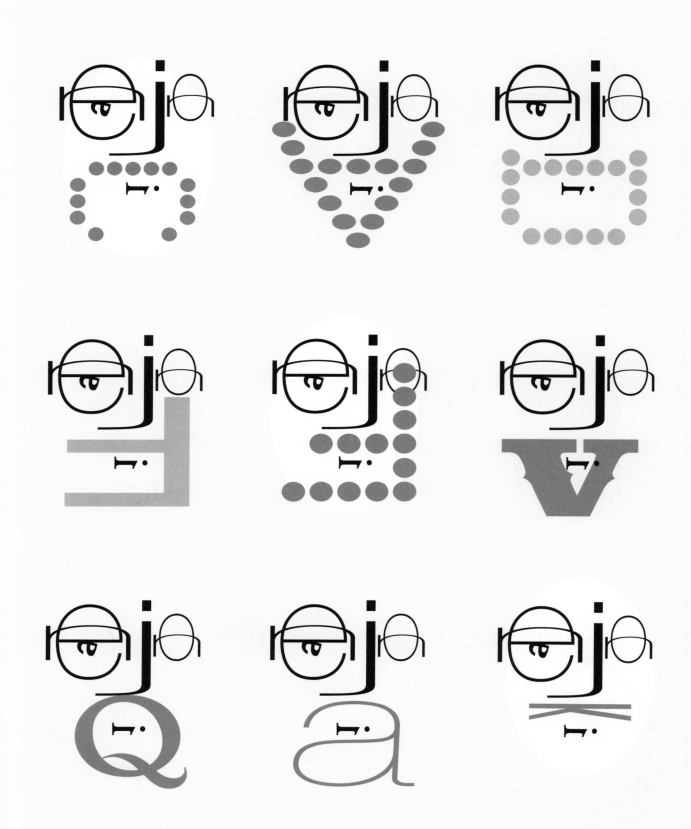

Made from ejonai plus CADFFvQal

The fonts should match the *personality* of the subject.
The **Gothic** letter 'n' (𝖓) makes dark eyes for this beatnik character,
and a bold, rounded H (**H**) makes a great turtle-neck sweater.

Tim MincHiN

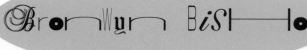

Letter Art can be complex or simple; realistic or abstract. See which letters inspire you or **resemble** features like:

nose
mouth
ears
teeth
+
forehead
cheeks
chin
neck
wrinkles
shoulders
hands
+
eyebrows
eyelashes
hair
moustache
beard
fringe
baldness
+
hat
collar
tie
jewellery
glasses
pipe...

Try to find the **perfect** font to reflect the *style* of the person:
Are they elegant, spiky, chunky, quirky, classical, modern, gothic, western...?

Can you find these eyes and mouths throughout this book?

Whether *famous* or *family*, the key to a portrait is **expression**... it puts the *life* into a face. What letters can you find in this face?

Bonjour! Je *rock* le monde!

JuLiA ZEmiro

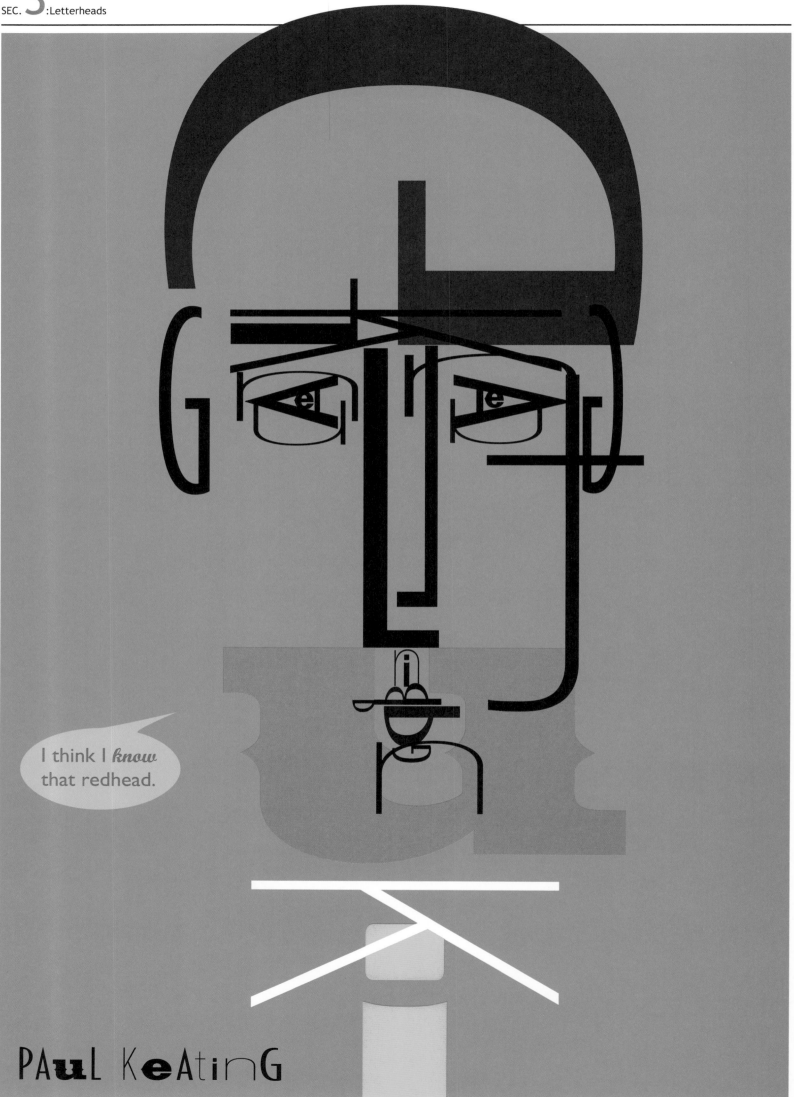

EXTRA HARD

The hardest portraits use only the *exact letters* of a *one-word name*... **no** extra fonts, and **no** extra letter repeats!

YIKES! Is that possible?

Anything's possible in design!

Diana

georgie

MeLissa

MArgArEt

neLLie

marLene

DAVid

DiaNe

biLLY

Now for some famous **cowboys**, INDIANS and *pirates*...

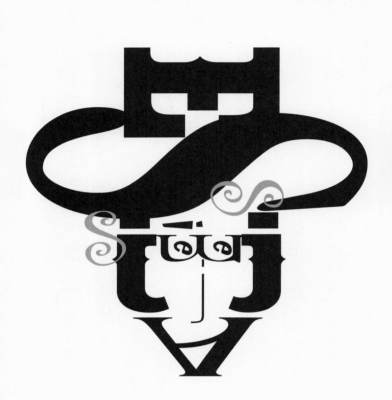

jeSSie jAmES

Annie OAKLey

★ CORRECT SPELLING ★ Each portrait is made *using only the letters of the character's name.* Repeat letters if you like. {A hat is a great way to start a portrait}.

BLue BeaRD

CAPtAIn jACK

Can you find these letters of my name hidden in my portrait?

geroniMo!

DaVID GULPiLLiL

Can you find the letters that spell these famous Indigenous Australians?

tRUganiNi

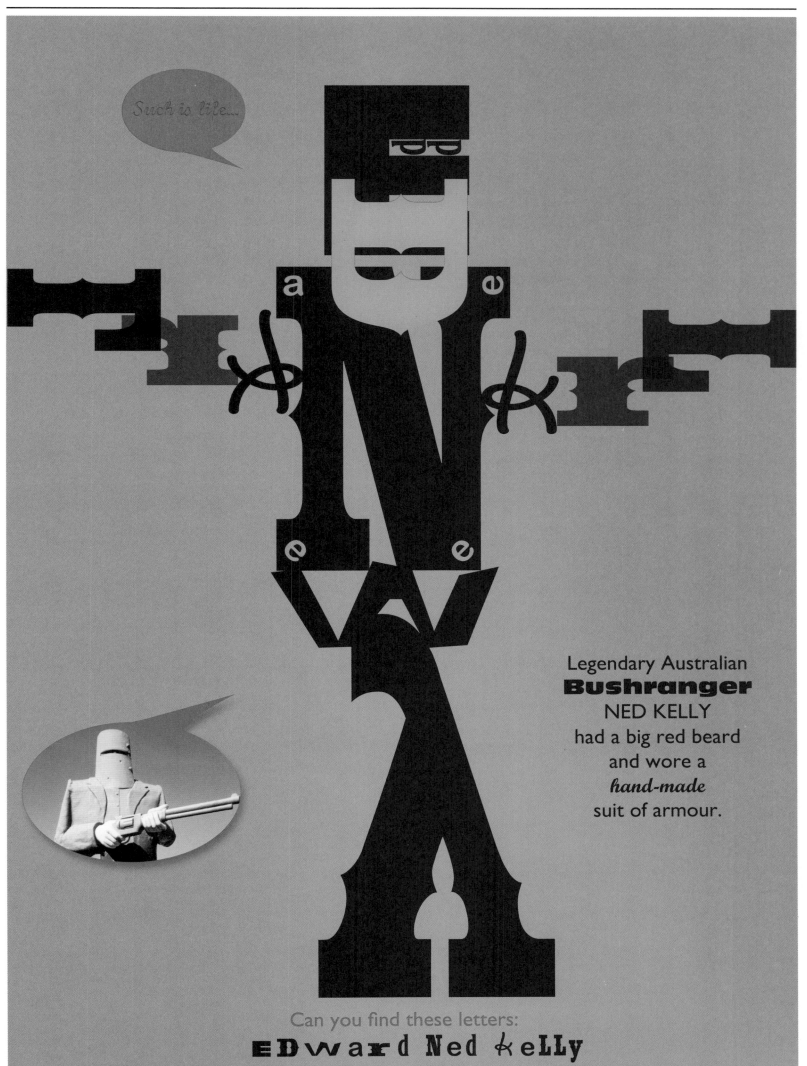

CAPTAIN HOOK

NAPOLEON BonAPArte

Historic figures have unusual *costumes* and *uniforms* that will add graphic interest to a Letter Art portrait. Get to know your local history and folklore.

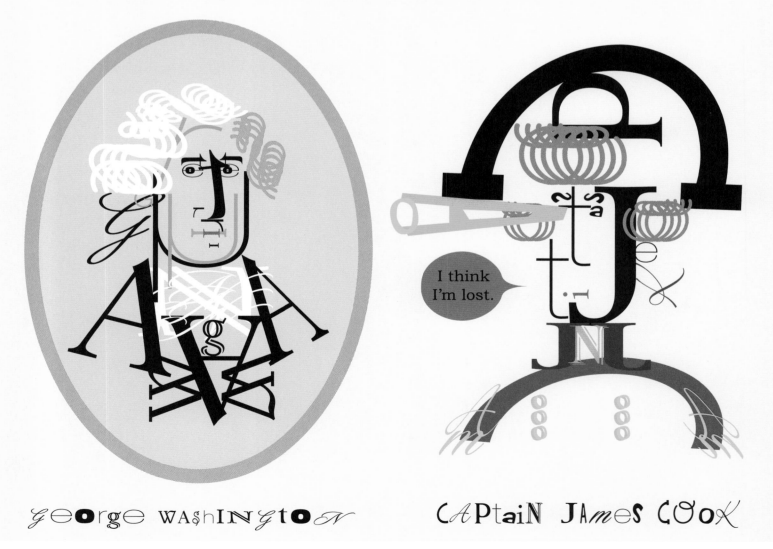

I think I'm lost.

GEOrge WAShINGtoN

CAPtaiN JAmeS COoK

The careful use
of *colour*
makes a big difference
to the portrait.

How very puzzling.

My portrait is made with:
aLBert EiNSteiN

Can you spell me?
Find the letters of my name:

eMpreSS CLeopatra

Whether the portrait is realistic or abstract, **match** the fonts to the *personality*.

...Am I Woman?

Can you spell me, possums?

DAme eDnA eVerAGe

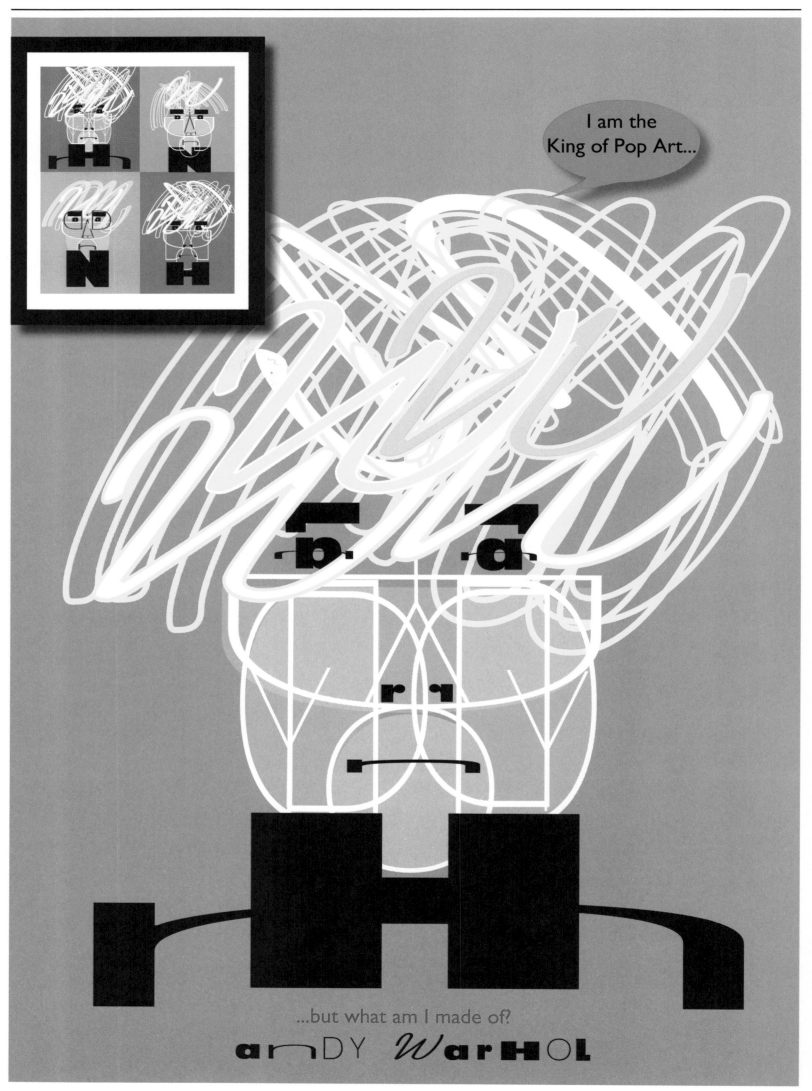

American
President
Number 16,
Abraham
Lincoln...

Can you find these
letters in my face:

AbraHam LIncoLn

...and Number 44, President Obama is made from:

PrESiDENt OBaMa

I'm the King of *Rock'n'roll*

eLVis PrEsLEy

A *caricature* is a simplified portrait
like a cartoon, that captures
the essence of a likeness,
often with *exaggerated* features.

I'm the King of *Pop*

MichaeL JacKSon

Unscramble these portraits to spell the names of...

KyLIE minoguE

Spanish artist **Pablo Picasso** *re-arranged* facial features to create his *abstract* portraits. Can you find the letters that make his name?

PABLO PiCASSO

Mexican artist **Frida Kahlo** had a tiny pale *moustache* and thick *eyebrows* that joined together above her nose. She painted lots of self-portraits featuring traditional hairstyles, jewellery, and often with a *chimp* or a *cat* on her shoulder.

FriDa KAHLO

chimp

Frida KAHLo Cat+Chimp

Mona lisa

The best portraits become **iconic**. That means they become the most popular image of that person. They are reproduced and imitated *over and over again* throughout history... like the portraits of *The New Yorker* dandy or the Mona Lisa.

tHε nεw yorkεr

THE NEW YORKER

IMAGE CREDITS:
All photographs by M.Coote unless otherwise attributed:
p.24 *LONDON EYE* (Creative Commons) Photo by Kham Tran, 2009. www.khamtran.com
p.25 *CHRYSLER BUILDING RETOUCHED* (Creative Commons) Photos by David Shankbone, 2009.
p.31 *BIG BEN, PALACE OF WESTMINSTER, LONDON* Photo by Ginger Ridgeway, 2015.
p.36 *SYDNEY HARBOUR BRIDGE AUSTRALIA,* (Creative Commons) Photo by Redlegsfan2, 2014.
    Modified by M.Coote 2015.
p.37 *EIFFEL TOWER DAY SEPT 2005 (10),*(Creative Commons) Photo by Kscolan, 2005.
p.39 *LUNA PARK IN ST KILDA* (Creative Commons) Photo by Bidgee, 2014. Modified by M.Coote 2015.
p.101 *GEORGE WASHINGTON* by Gilbert Stuart, 1795.
p.102 *ALBERT EINSTEIN* (Creative Commons) by Orin Jack Turner, 1947. Modified by M. Coote 2015.
p.107 *DAME EDNA EVERAGE,* Wikimedia/Creative Commons & Megastar Productions.
p.110 *THE GETTYSBURG PORTRAIT* by Alexander Gardner, 1863. Modified by M.Coote, 2015.
p.111 *OBAMA HOPE* (Detail) by Shepard Fairey/Obeygiant.com
p.118 (Top): *MONA LISA* by Leonardo da Vinci, c1517;
    (Bottom): *THE NEW YORKER* cover, first edition: illustration by Rea Irwin, 1925.

ACKNOWLEDGEMENTS AND GRATEFUL THANKS TO:
Megan Ellis for production; Lena Frew and C+C for printing; Marilen Tabacco for creative liaison;
Ginger Ridgeway, Stefano Boscutti and Jacqueline Young for edits and checks; Lex Ridgeway for everything.